Contents

Egg hunt

Can you guess what is underneath these leaves?

Life as a
Butterfly

Vic Parker

Heinemann

GW 2430056 X

Little Nippers

www.heinemann.co.uk/library
Visit our website to find out more information about **Heinemann Library** books.

To order:
☎ Phone 44 (0) 1865 888066
▤ Send a fax to 44 (0) 1865 314091
▱ Visit the Heinemann Bookshop at www.heinemann.co.uk/library to browse our catalogue and order online.

First published in Great Britain by Heinemann Library, Halley Court, Jordan Hill, Oxford OX2 8EJ, part of Harcourt Education.
Heinemann is a registered trademark of Harcourt Education Ltd.

Editorial: Jilly Attwood and Claire Throp
Design: Jo Hinton-Malivoire and bigtop, Bicester, UK
Models made by: Jo Brooker
Picture Research: Catherine Bevan
Production: Séverine Ribierre

Originated by Dot Gradations
Printed and bound in China by South China Printing Company

ISBN 0 431 17101 7 (hardback)
07 06 05 04 03
10 9 8 7 6 5 4 3 2 1

ISBN 0 431 17106 8 (paperback)
07 06 05 04 03
10 9 8 7 6 5 4 3 2 1

British Library Cataloguing in Publication Data
Parker, Vic
Life as a butterfly
595.7'89
A full catalogue record for this book is available from the British Library.

Acknowledgements
The publishers would like to thank the following for permission to reproduce photographs:
Andy Purcell p. **14**; Bruce Coleman pp. **12**, **17** (Kim Taylor), **16** (Petr Zabransky); FLPA pp. **15** (Roger Wilmshurst), **20** (Heather Angel); Holt Studios pp. **5**, **7** (Nigel Cattlin); Mark N Boulton p. **4**; NHPA pp. **18-19**, **22**, **23**; NHPA pp. **11**, **13** (Stephen Dalton); NHPA/Image Quest 3-D p. **9**; Oxford Scientific Films pp. **6**, **10**; OSF p. **21** (Barrie Watts), **8** (Tony Allen).

Cover photograph reproduced with permission of OSF/London Scientific Films

The publishers would like to thank Annie Davy for her assistance in the preparation of this book.

Every effort has been made to contact copyright holders of any material reproduced in this book. Any omissions will be rectified in subsequent printings if notice is given to the publishers.

egg

Lots and lots of tiny eggs!

A munching machine

A very hungry caterpillar is hatching from one of these eggs.

The caterpillar eats and eats and grows and grows and eats and eats and grows and grows.

Pupa

After four or five weeks, it makes a shell called a pupa around itself.

Some **big** changes happen inside.

From crawling to flying

The caterpillar changes into a butterfly!

First the butterfly dries its wings
in the sun.

Feeding time

Then it flutters away for the very first time.

The butterfly finds food
inside flowers.

tongue

It sucks up a sugary juice called
nectar with its *long* tongue.

Finding a home

Butterflies live wherever flowers grow.

Small tortoiseshell butterfly

Peacock butterfly

Butterfly wings

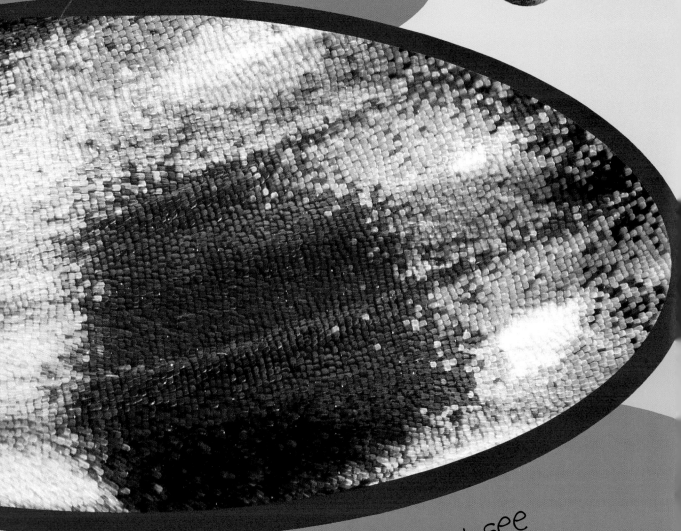

What colours can you see in the butterfly's wings?

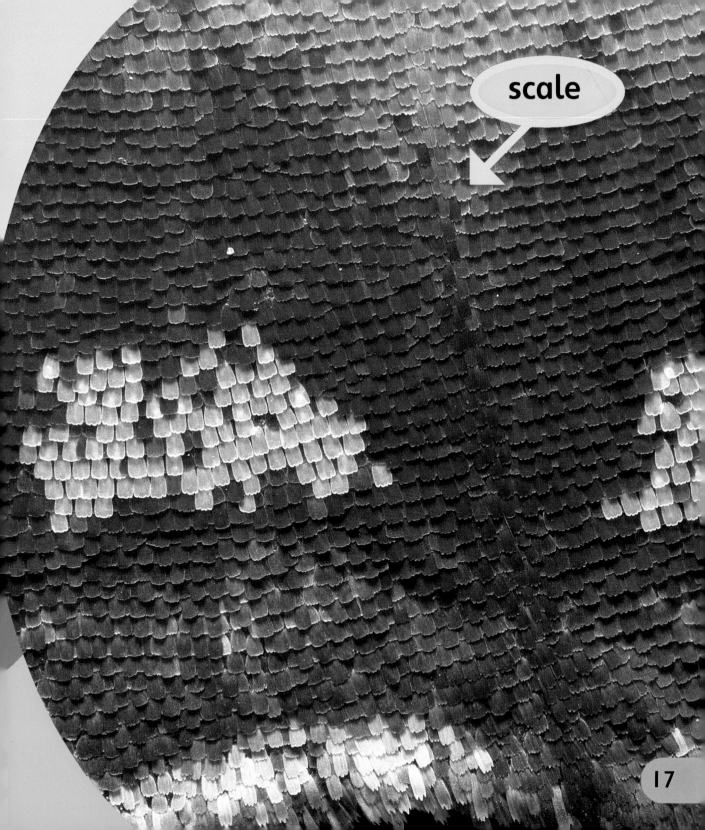

scale

Sleeping

In winter some butterflies fly away to sunnier countries.

Others sleep for the whole winter!

Meeting a mate

When a female and male butterfly meet they dance around each other in the air.

Then they hide away together in the bushes.

Butterfly babies

The female butterfly flies off to lay eggs.

Index

The end

Notes for adults

The **Life as a** . . . series looks at the life cycles of familiar animals and plants, introducing the young child to the concept of change over time. There are four titles in the series and when used together, they will enable comparison of similarities and differences between life cycles. The key curriculum early learning goals relevant to this series are:
Knowledge and understanding of the world
   – find out about, and identify, some features of living things that the young child observes
   – ask questions about why things happen
   – differentiate between past and present.

This book takes the reader on a circular journey from the beginning of a butterfly's life as an egg, through its developmental stages (including habitat and what the caterpillar needs to grow), to maturity and reproduction. The book will help children extend their vocabulary, as they will hear new words such as *pupa* and *nectar*. You might like to introduce the word *hibernate* when reading to children that some butterflies sleep for the whole winter. It will be helpful to explain to young readers that many of the photographs are much larger than life size.

Additional information about butterflies
Butterflies are insects – a group of creatures that have three distinct body parts (head, thorax and abdomen), six legs, and usually wings at some stage of their life, which are covered in scales. There are more species of insect than any other creature on Earth. Butterflies are more active by day than moths (which are usually active by night), and butterflies are more brightly coloured. There are more than 15,000 kinds of butterfly.

Follow-up activities
• In local parks and gardens, look for butterfly eggs, caterpillars and pupae.
• Visit a butterfly farm.
• Make a collage of a butterfly from different coloured paper or sweet wrappers.